Copyright © Graffeg 2011
ISBN 9781905582556

Cooks & Kids.
Written by Alan Rustad &
Andrew Isaac.
Photography © National
Fostering Agency Limited.

Graffeg,
Radnor Court,
256 Cowbridge Road East,
Cardiff CF5 1GZ Wales UK.
Tel: +44 (0)29 2078 5156
sales@graffeg.com
www.graffeg.com

Graffeg are hereby identified
as the authors of this work in
accordance with section 77 of
the Copyrights, Designs and
Patents Act 1988.

Distributed by the Welsh Books
Council www.cllc.org.uk
castellbrychan@cllc.org.uk

A CIP Catalogue record for this
book is available from the
British Library.

Designed and produced by
Peter Gill & Associates
sales@petergill.com
www.petergill.com

National Fostering Agency Ltd
Frays Court
71 Cowley Road
Uxbridge
Middlesex, UB8 2AE
Tel: 01895 200 300
www.nfa.ws
cooks&kids@nfa.ws

Graffeg and the National
Fostering Agency would like to
thank the following companies
for their invaluable support:

De Vere Venues
For providing all of the
ingredients, facilities and
chefs during the cooking
photoshoots.

STEEL London
For designing and building our
Cooks & Kids website –
www.cooksandkids.com

Sodexo
For providing the important
nutritional information for
children in the book.

WRG
For support with video and
media production.

The publishers are also
grateful to the Welsh Books
Council for their financial
support and marketing advice.
www.gwales.com

Cooks & Kids is a registered
trademark.

11 top chefs and children cook up a storm in the kitchen with their favourite recipes.

GRAFFEG

Cooks & Kids

Contents

Macie's fairy cakes

children are the heart of everything we do

Foreword
Iain Anderson

It is a pleasure to welcome you to our book, Cooks & Kids, which is the National Fostering Agency's debut in book publishing.

The National Fostering Agency is the second largest independent fostering agency in the UK and is totally committed to improving the quality of life for children and young people in our care. Children and young people in society today face many problems as they move from childhood to adulthood and I am extremely proud of the hard work and dedication that our carers give to the 1,800 plus children and young people that we look after throughout the United Kingdom.

As adults move towards living longer it is important that children and young people have a balanced and healthy diet in their early years. As we are all aware, fast food, junk and processed food have little or no nutritional value and can have a detrimental effect on an individual's health.

Cooks & Kids aims to redress the balance. Yes there will always be foods that can be regarded as "treats" and we make no apology for including those recipes in this book. Food should be fun, food should be enjoyable and more importantly, food should play a key role in a healthy diet. Therefore also included are some nutritious dishes that not only taste good but are great fun to make. The pictures and recipes contained within the book clearly show how our young chefs thoroughly enjoyed themselves being creative in the kitchen working with professionals.

I would like to thank the large team of people – chefs, social workers, and of course, the children and young people – for allowing the project to take off and evolve into this cookery book. I would also like to thank Tony Dangerfield, COO of De Vere Venues for all the help he has given my team and the superb commitment and dedication shown by his chefs and managers during the photo shoots. From page 92 onwards you will find a full list of all those individuals and organisations who have supported and contributed to making this happen. My thanks also go to our top chefs for agreeing to participate and having lots of fun in doing so.

We are delighted that the royalties from the sales of this book will go to the Magic Breakfast to help them in the valuable work they do in schools to ensure children can start each day with a healthy meal. In schools with more than 50 per cent free school meals, too many children start the day too hungry to learn. A hungry child is often unable to concentrate in class. Good nutrition makes a positive impact on learning.

I hope you will take pleasure in reading this book and just as importantly try to prepare the recipes the youngsters created for you – enjoy.

Iain Anderson

Chief Executive Officer
National Fostering Agency

National Fostering Agency

Founded in 1995, the National Fostering Agency (NFA) provides high quality foster care that places children and young people at the heart of everything they do.

NFA works with local authorities and foster carers to create the best possible opportunities and outcomes for children. It is the foster care provider of choice for many local authorities across the UK. NFA employs experienced and professionally qualified staff and only recruits the highest quality foster carers, providing effective, ongoing training to develop skills and knowledge. Programmes are implemented to monitor and manage each foster care placement, working to each child's individually tailored care plan. Foster carers have access to social workers 24 hours a day, seven days a week.

The team at NFA is totally committed to the improvement of outcomes for every child it looks after and can demonstrate the real impact of the care it provides. Outcomes and individual placement recordings for each child are securely recorded and the information is freely available to all placing authorities.

NFA is proud to collaborate with so many loyal and dedicated foster carers, without whom the service would not exist. Partnering with its long serving carers and its dedicated professional team NFA is proud to add to the quality of daily life for those children and young people in its care.

If you want to learn more about being a foster carer call 0845 200 40 40 or visit www.nfa.ws

Magic Breakfast

Magic Breakfast is a UK registered charity, dedicated to ensuring every child starts their school day with the right breakfast as fuel for learning.

The royalties from Cooks & Kids go to the Magic Breakfast charity. They provide free healthy breakfast food to schools with over 50% free school meals to reach the hungriest children. Every day, together with a strong network of corporate partners, individuals and schools, Magic Breakfast gives over 6000 children the best start to the day. What better outcome for the fruits of this fun and creative project than to 'pass on' the kindness and dedication of others

to make a practical and tangible difference to someone else, each and every day. There are 3.9 million children living in poverty in the UK (defined as 60% below the average income) and research from Child Poverty Action indicates that their school lunch is the only hot meal for 1 in 4. An astounding 32% of school children regularly miss breakfast, and up to 700,000 children arrive at school too hungry to learn every day. **www.magicbreakfast.com**

7

children are the heart of everything we do

Introduction

Cooks & Kids was born out of a passion for food and a fun way to engage children and young people in wonderful tastes and food combinations. How do you ever encourage young people to think about food, what is good for them and more importantly to have a go at actually preparing something to eat?

The National Fostering Agency (NFA) is as proud as it can possibly be of the outcomes of the children and young people in its care and is always seeking ways to enable looked after children and the birth children of its carers to contribute to the key tenets of 'Every Child Matters'

- be healthy
- stay safe
- enjoy and achieve
- make a positive contribution
- achieve economic well-being

Cooks & Kids 'ticks the box' on a number of these, particularly making a positive contribution. Looked after children in foster care do not want to be labelled, they want a normal life, to take part in everyday normal things and most of all want to be in a caring environment. Understanding and being informed about food, however small a part it may play, is a route where children and young people can be encouraged to take control, make decisions and be creative.

Preparing food for others is a great way to show how much you care and this is probably what made Cooks & Kids work as an idea. It has enabled the professional world of top chefs

and NFA's fostered and birth children engage with each other, have huge amounts of fun and work together to create the book, helping disadvantaged children.

Making Cooks & Kids worthwhile beyond the achievement of participation and engagement with NFA's children and young people needed careful consideration. Getting the project off the ground was not a simple task, and particularly as at NFA we were determined to take a 'time and talent' approach. This was to ensure the ethos of Cooks & Kids might genuinely be achieved by companies and professionals supporting the project through a belief that Cooks & Kids could, and would, make a difference.

Using the contacts made by myself and our Chief Executive, Iain Anderson, my co-author Alan and I set about encouraging some well-known chefs to participate. At the same time, the recipe hunt was launched throughout the extended NFA family of children, young people and birth children. Over subsequent weeks dozens of recipes came in from all over the country, creative, funny, exciting, indulgent, tasty – all of them carefully crafted and written down by youngsters of varying abilities and knowledge. Appreciating some of the challenges facing some of these young people is heart rending, and to hear the stories from social workers and carers on how, even at this stage, taking part in Cooks & Kids had already made a difference to the youngsters involved.

The help of John Woodward, Executive Head Chef for De Vere Venues was enlisted to help sort the recipes into a practical and workable series of dishes that could become part of a cookbook for kids and by kids. De Vere kindly offered to host the photo shoots and John and his team of award-winning chefs set about pairing up with the youngsters and creating a series of dishes the youngsters would be asked to prepare in addition to their own recipe.

At the same time, our top chefs were contacting us, wanting to be part of this great project whether it be providing their own recipes to go into the cook book, coaching one of the young people or coming along to one of the photo shoots to cook!!

After many months, Cooks & Kids was coming together, professional photographers Miranda, Simon, Lisa and Martin had all volunteered their time for three very hectic photo shoots.

Steel volunteered to create the website and the brilliant De Vere guys sorted all the ingredients and loaned us some real kitchens for the day.

In all honesty, I have never seen such fun had by so many for such a long time and the resultant food was amazing. From little Macie's fairy cakes to Rebecca's dahl and almonds to Alyssa's dairy-free apricot rock cakes and Dylan's sunday leftovers risotto, they all tasted fantastic.

The support and feedback from everyone we have approached during the course of this project has been remarkable. Without exception, everyone has been enthusiastic and offered assistance in a variety of ways. We are grateful to them all.

So please enter the spirit of how Cooks & Kids came about. Cooking is fun. Fun food does not have to be junk food. Just try these recipes. And of course if you have a recipe you feel we should throw into the pot for the future, just let us know. For us "too many cooks" does not apply, the more the merrier!

Bon appétit.

Alan Andrew

children are the heart of everything we do

De Vere Venues

A cornerstone for the business, the De Vere Group is 'Fanatical about Food' and delivering a first class food and beverage service for its customers across its hotel and venue portfolio.

A fantastic opportunity to be involved with the National Fostering Agency and Cooks & Kids, John Woodward leapt at the chance to get involved.

John and the team at De Vere have heavily supported this excellent initiative by inviting some of the children to three special cookery days. Held at several of the Group's properties: Cameron House in Scotland, Holborn Bars in London and Staverton Park in Northamptonshire, the children were invited to submit their own recipe ideas before coming along to cook them in person with John and his team of chefs.

Keen to share his knowledge and passion for good food, John and his team gave the children an inspirational and fun day learning about cooking before sitting down to enjoy their own dishes for lunch. Delighted to make a small difference by being able to give the children a positive and exciting experience of working in a professional kitchen, the team at De Vere was richly rewarded by the children's eagerness to learn and enthusiasm.

De Vere Group is the UK's leading independent hotel and hospitality group. Offering business and leisure travellers refreshingly different hotels and venues with a modern British flavour, De Vere Group is made up of De Vere Venues, Hotels and VILLAGE. With 65 properties ranging from beautiful listed country houses, championship-level golf resorts, city-based business centres and unique venues; De Vere offers impeccable service and expertise. With an elite team, state of the art technology and equipment, acres of outdoor space, impressive and award-winning signature restaurants and guest accommodation, De Vere leads the way in terms of space for the business and leisure tourist.

Contact details

For more information about the De Vere Group of companies please contact visit www.devere.co.uk. For event enquiries please contact the team on 0844 980 8054 or for reservations please telephone: De Vere Venues – 0844 980 0233, De Vere Hotels – 0844 980 9950 and De Vere VILLAGE on 0844 980 0220.

Cameron House, Scotland

Keeping safe in the kitchen

Before you begin cooking:

- It is dangerous to cook without proper supervision – always ask the permission of your foster carer/parent before cooking.
- Make sure the floor isn't wet otherwise you could slip over and hurt yourself.
- Keep pets out of the kitchen when preparing food.
- Keep all work and storage areas clean – clean all worktops before and after use. This is important if you have been using raw meat, poultry, fish or unwashed vegetables.
- Make sure to wash and dry your hands before handling any food or cooking utensils. Wash your hands with soap and water, not just water!
- Make sure to wash all of your food by rinsing it under the tap before cooking.
- Ensure all food is within its 'best before' date.

While you're cooking:

- Prepare and store raw meat separately – use a different knife and chopping board.

- Once you've finished handling the raw meat make sure to wash your hands thoroughly. Don't touch any other surfaces before you wash your hands or you could spread the bacteria.
- Make sure any pots and pans handles are turned inward and not overhanging the edge, otherwise you could knock them over.

When you've finished cooking:

- Make sure all food is cooked properly – if you're not sure, check with an adult.
- Never eat food that has uncooked eggs in it.
- Check labels and packaging to see how long it is safe to store foods once their packaging has been opened.
- Make sure all of your food is stored in a cool dry place or in a fridge/freezer, this will stop the growth of bacteria and germs.
- Store food at the correct temperature. Food could 'go off' and not be suitable for eating.
- Make sure all food is well wrapped before it goes in the fridge or freezer.

- Always keep raw meat on the bottom shelf of your fridge to stop any drips contaminating other food.
- Don't put open canned food in the fridge, the food could react with the aluminium in the can and go off. Transfer the food into a plastic container.

Germs and bacteria are invisible

- Food poisoning can be caused by bacteria, viruses, metals, chemicals or poisonous plants: remember if food has been contaminated it will taste and smell the same as it normally would. One of the main causes of food poisoning is from improper food storage, or incorrectly prepared (undercooked) food.

Danger in the Kitchen

Kitchens can be dangerous if you don't take care – watch out for:

- sharp knives
- hot pans and hobs
- and definitely no running at any time in the kitchen!

Nutrition

Nutrition and healthy eating

To stay healthy it is important we get the right balance of nutrients from a variety of different foods throughout the day.

There are no good or bad foods. All foods and drinks will provide some form of nutrients and energy, but we need to understand the types and proportions needed to achieve a healthy and well balanced diet.

We should identify the types and proportions of foods we eat in a day from five food groups. This should include all meals and snacks.

What are the five food groups?

The five food groups are:

- Fruit and vegetables
- Bread, rice, potatoes, pasta and other starchy foods
- Meat, fish, eggs, beans and non dairy sources of protein
- Milk and dairy foods
- Foods and drinks high in fat and/or sugar

Fruit and vegetables

Fruit and vegetables provide us with vitamins, minerals and fibre. This group of foods are generally low in fat, that is unless we add fats and oils during cooking or cover them with a rich sauce.

A third of all the foods we eat should come from fruits and vegetables. This is equivalent to having at least 5 portions a day. These can be fresh, canned, dried, frozen or juiced.

Top tip: add variety to the fruit or vegetables you eat by eating a rainbow of colours. Why not try a new fruit or vegetable every week.

Bread, rice, potatoes, pasta and other starchy foods

This group of foods are high in starchy carbohydrates and provide us with lots of energy. Energy is important for growth and development, and for everyday activities. They also provide us with some calcium, iron and B vitamins.

Top tip: non sugar-coated wholegrain cereals are better for you than the sugared ones.

oily fish contain a fatty acid known as omega-3.

Meat, fish, eggs, beans and non dairy sources of protein

This group of foods are high in protein, needed for the repair and growth of body cells. They can also be rich in iron, especially red meats such as beef, lamb or pork. One sixth of all the foods we eat should come from this group.

Oily fish such as salmon, tuna, mackerel, sardines and trout all contain a fatty acid known as omega-3.

Top tip: choose leaner cuts of meat and remove any visible fat. Always remove skin from chicken and other poultry.

Milk and dairy foods

Milk and dairy foods such as cheeses and yogurts are high in protein and calcium. Calcium is important for maintaining strong bones and teeth.

Like meat, fish, eggs and beans, one sixth of all the

foods we eat should come from this group.

Top tip: 1 glass of milk will contribute around ½ to ⅓ of your daily requirement of calcium

Foods and drinks high in fat and/or sugar

Foods high in fat and or sugar include sweets, chocolates, fizzy drinks, cakes, biscuits, crisps. These provide us with lots of energy and if eaten in large quantities will give us more energy than we need. This will then contribute towards being overweight.

This group should only be eaten in very small amounts. This is no more than to one twelfth of the total foods we eat in a day.

Top tip: try snacking on dried fruit instead of crisps and chocolate.

Fluid and hydration

It is also important that you remember to drink plenty of fluids such as water, fresh fruit juice, smoothies or milk. Carry a bottle of water with you throughout the day to keep well hydrated and don't forget to drink more during hot weather, warm environments and after any physical activity.

Do I really need breakfast?

When getting ready for school in the morning, breakfast might not seem like the most important thing on your mind, but in fact a healthy breakfast is a great way to kick start your day.

Tucking into a healthy breakfast!

A healthy breakfast can simply be a slice of toast with jam, peanut butter or just plainly toasted with a thin spreading of margarine.

Why not try something different like bagels or breakfast muffins instead of toast or cereals.

Other breakfast ideas:

- start the day with a refreshing glass of fresh milk (preferably skimmed or semi-skimmed) or a glass of fruit juice
- make a fruit smoothie with a handful of your favourite fruits
- add a couple of tablespoons of low fat yoghurt or a handful of dried fruits to your cereals
- a warm bowl of porridge could be brightened up with berries such as blueberries, blackberries or strawberries

Remember, a good healthy breakfast is just as important at the weekends and during holidays.

Source: Sodexo. See page 93.

Fruit and vegetables provide us with vitamins, minerals and fibre.

Cooks & Kids

Kent-born Chris Lee and his wife Hayley run the award-winning The Bildeston Crown. Chris attained a 3 AA Rosette status and was named an 'up-and-coming' chef in the Good Food Guide. Recently he has won Suffolk Restaurant of the Year.

Chris Lee

The Bildeston Crown

Top Chefs

De Vere

John Woodward

John is the Executive Head Chef for De Vere Venues, and helped all of our budding chefs during the Cooks & Kids cookery days. Fanatical about food, John has had a diverse career; starting under acclaimed chefs such as the Roux brothers before travelling and working in Australia and operating in the venue sector.

Tom Kerridge is chef-patron at The Hand & Flowers in Marlow. Before this, Tom worked at London restaurants including Odette's and The Capital. Tom is a regular on food television and is the only chef to have cooked at the finalists banquet twice on BBC 2's Great British Menu.

Tom Kerridge

The Hand & Flowers

Fishmonger, food writer, restaurateur. Mitch Tonks is widely regarded as a champion of great British seafood. He has 3 restaurants — RockFish Grill & Seafood Market, The Seahorse, and RockFish Seafood and Chips.

Mitch Tonks

The Seahorse

Shaun Rankin

Bohemia

Yorkshire-born Shaun Rankin has worked in restaurants as close to home as Darlington and as far afield as Chicago and Australia. He has now made his home in Jersey, the largest of the Channel Islands. He is head chef of Bohemia, part of the Club Hotel & Spa, and has retained a Michelin Star for 7 years.

Hailing from Denbigh in North Wales, over the last ten years Bryn has worked under Marco Pierre-White at The Criterion, Michel Roux at Le Gavroche, was Senior-Sous at The Orrery and opened Galvin at Windows with Chris Galvin, before opening Odette's in 2006 and then buying the restaurant himself in 2008.

Bryn Williams

Odette's

Cooks & Kids

Matt Tebbutt runs The Foxhunter, near Abergavenny, serving modern British cooking. Matt presents Market Kitchen's Big Adventure on UKTV and guest-presents Saturday Kitchen on BBC1. He provides recipes and features for a variety of magazines and has written a cookbook of his favourite dishes – Matt Tebbutt Cooks Country.

Matt Tebbutt

The Foxhunter

West One

Gill Moss

Gill is the sous chef at De Vere Whites hotel where she has worked for 11 years. She always wanted to become a chef and had a great time cooking with the kids for this book. The dishes she cooked were simple and healthy but also interesting for children to make.

Stephen learnt his craft at several of London's top restaurants, including Marco Pierre White's first restaurant Harvey's and Michel Roux's Le Gavroche. He earned a Michelin star for the Canteen restaurant in London at the age of 25, and opened The Hardwick restaurant in Abergavenny in 2005.

Stephen Terry

The Hardwick

Lisa Allen is Head Chef at the Northcote, retaining the restaurant's Michelin Star status since 2005. She was the first female chef to reach the final of BBC2's Great British Menu, cooking for Prince Charles, and this year she reached the final stages of the competition again.

Lisa Allen

Northcote

Atul Kochhar

Benares

Atul Kochhar has re-invented Indian cuisine, becoming the first Indian chef to receive a Michelin star. He then opened Benares, where his creative talents were awarded, again with a Michelin star in 2007. In 2004, Atul published his successful debut recipe book, Indian Essence. His third book, Curries of the World, will be published in autumn 2012.

children are the heart of everything we do

Rebecca, 16, gave us her recipe for delicious Indian vegetarian dahl. Rebecca likes to keep up the heat in the kitchen, with her most successful dish being a very hot curry for her brother with three different chilli powders in it.

Rebecca

Atul Kochhar

Rebecca & Atul

Tomato and lentil dahl with toasted almonds

Atul was the first Indian chef to receive a Michelin star, and is famous for his own brand of Indian cookery. He has written three cookbooks and runs the kitchen of Benares restaurant in London.

Stirring the mixture to prevent burning.

The best part! Eating all my hard work.

Chef's comments

This is a great Indian recipe that can be paired with any vegetable, fish or meat that you like! This dish also acts as a great side dish to accompany any meal. Don't forget the chillies if you prefer it spicy!

Atul Kochhar

children are the heart of everything we do

Rebecca & Atul

Tomato and lentil dahl with toasted almonds

Coriander

Red lentils

For 4 people
70 minutes cooking time
....

Ingredients

30ml/2 tbsp vegetable oil
1 large onion, finely chopped
3 garlic cloves, finely chopped
1 carrot, diced
10ml/2 tsp cumin seeds
10ml/2 tsp yellow mustard seeds
2.5m/1 inch fresh ginger root, grated
10ml/2 tsp ground tumeric
5ml/1 tsp mild chilli powder
5ml/1 tsp garam masala
225g/8oz/1 cup split red lentils
400ml/1 and two third cups water
400ml/1 and two third cups coconut milk
5 tomatoes, peeled, seeded and chopped
Juice of 2 limes
60ml/4 tbsp chopped fresh coriander
Salt and freshly ground black pepper
25g/1oz/¼ cup flaked almonds toasted
   to serve

Tomato and lentil dahl with toasted almonds

Tomato and lentil dahl with toasted almonds

Method

1 Heat the oil in a large heavy-based saucepan. Sauté the onion for 5 minutes until softened, stirring occasionally.

2 Add the garlic, carrot, cumin, mustard seeds and ginger. Cook for 5 minutes stirring until the seeds begin to pop and the carrots softens slightly.

3 Stir in the ground tumeric, chilli powder and garam masala, and cook for 1 minute or until the flavours begin to mingle. Stir to prevent the spices burning.

4 Add the lentils, water, coconut milk and tomatoes. Season well.

5 Bring to the boil, then reduce the heat, cover and simmer for about 45 minutes. Stir occasionally to prevent the lentils sticking. Stir in the lime juice and 45ml/3 tbsp of the fresh coriander, then season to taste.

6 Cook for a further 5 minutes until the lentils soften and become tender. To serve, sprinkle on top with the remaining coriander and the flaked almonds.

Grating the ginger root.

Plating up the dahl.

A final drizzle of oil and done.

children are the heart of everything we do

Georgia, 12, made this dish because it is chocolatey and served with ice cream it's all the more yummy! The cake would be perfect for a birthday party, and is a great dish to cook with friends to share.

Georgia Sutherland-Jones

Bryn Williams

Georgia & Bryn
Chocolate cake

Chocolate cake

Welsh chef Bryn has worked with some of London's top chefs, including Marco Pierre-White and Michel Roux, before opening his own restaurant Odette's to critical acclaim.

Putting the chocolate mixture into the dishes, ready for cooking in the oven for approximately 25 minutes.

Here I'm beating an egg into the creamed sugar and butter mixture, to bind the ingredients together and make the sponge.

Chef's comments

This is a great classic recipe, and one that adults enjoy just as much as kids. Georgia could also try warming the chocolate cake up, which would make a really delicious combination with the cold ice cream.

Bryn Williams

children are the heart of everything we do°

Georgia & Bryn

Chocolate cake

Plain chocolate

For 6 people
20–25 minutes cooking time

Ingredients

3 beaten eggs
175g unsalted butter (softened)
175g caster sugar
½ tsp baking powder
3 tbsp cocoa powder
150g self-raising flour
Butter for greasing

For the topping

100g milk chocolate
100g plain chocolate
200ml double cream

Milk chocolate

Georgia's finished chocolate cake

Method

1 Preheat the oven to 180°C/Gas Mark 4/350°F. Grease the 10 inch tin and line the edges with butter. Cream the butter and sugar together in a bowl until they are light and fluffy and gradually beat in the egg.

2 Then sieve the flour, cocoa powder and baking powder into a bowl and then fold them into the creamed mixture.

3 Put the mixture into the tin and bake for 20 minutes. Check the cake to see if it is cooked, if not then cook for a little longer.

4 Once cooked, leave to cool slightly then turn out onto a baking tray.

5 Break the milk and plain chocolate into a bowl and melt them over a pan of simmering water.

6 Once done remove from the heat and leave to cool for 5 minutes. Add the double cream and stir to thicken. Leave for a few minutes.

7 Make sure the cake is completely cool before putting on the topping. Place all of the topping on the cake top and sides.

Weighing the unsalted butter.

Adding the baking powder to the flour and cocoa powder.

Folding the creamed mixture together.

children are the heart of everything we do

Macie, 6, likes her fairy cakes because they taste yummy. These have been her most successful recipe, and she had lots of fun cooking in the London kitchen. If she was stranded on a desert island, she would take fish fingers, ice cream, pork, grapes and bananas.

Macie French

Stephen Terry

Macie & Stephen

Fairy cakes

Stephen earned his first Michelin star at 25 and has worked in restaurants in London, Paris and St Tropez. After gaining a Michelin Star at The Walnut Tree, he opened The Hardwick, near Abergavenny.

Spooning the fairy cake mixture into cake cases on a baking tray.

Chef's comments

It's impossible for you to only have one! Perfect for sharing with all of your friends.

Having three young children myself I know these are perfect for parties. They can be customised with different sprinkles and you could flavour the icing with some melted chocolate or orange or lemon zest – you could even add some food colouring!

Stephen Terry

27

children are the heart of everything we do

Macie & Stephen

Fairy cakes

Makes 12

15 minutes cooking time

Ingredients

For the cake

4 oz self-raising flour

4 oz caster sugar

4 oz margarine

2 eggs

For the icing

4 oz butter

8oz icing sugar

3 drops vanilla essence

1-2 tbsp milk

Eggs

Paper cake cases

Method

1 Preheat the oven to 180°C/Gas Mark 4/350°F. Place all the cake ingredients into a bowl and mix together with a wooden spoon. Mix until creamy.

2 Place the mixture into paper cases evenly and put in the oven to bake for approximately 15 minutes or until golden and a little firm. Cool on a cooking tray for five minutes.

3 For the icing mix the butter and icing in a bowl and add the vanilla essence and milk.

4 To colour the icing, add a few drops of the desired food colouring.

5 Add the icing to the top of the cake and decorate the top with the toppings of your choice.

Sieving the cake ingredients together to form a smooth mixture.

Stirring the mixture together, make a wish!

Fairy cakes

Piping the icing onto the top of the cakes — just add toppings.

children are the heart of everything we do°

Amber, 14, submitted this recipe to Cooks & Kids saying she likes it because it is quick to make. Following in the footsteps of her favourite chefs Jamie Oliver, Heston Blumenthal and Levi Roots, Amber had a great time in the kitchen making this dish.

Amber

Atul Kochhar

Amber & Atul

Quickie pan-fried salmon

Atul was the first Indian chef to receive a Michelin star, and is famous for his own brand of Indian cookery. He has written three cookbooks and runs the kitchen of Benares restaurant in London.

Sprinkling all-purpose seasoning on the fillets.

It tastes as delicious as it looks!

Chef's comments

Salmon is a great choice as it is quick to make and it is a healthy choice. Try experimenting with the spices used on the salmon and find out what combination you like best. Salmon works well with sweet and savoury flavours!

Atul Kochhar

children are the heart of everything we do°

Amber & Atul

Quickie pan-fried salmon

For 4 people
20 minutes cooking time

Ingredients

4 skinless salmon fillets (150g each)
1 tbsp olive oil
1 tsp garlic paste
All purpose seasoning
Curry powder
Dried herbs de Provence
2 large carrots
100g broccoli
400g pasta
1 jar of pasta sauce

400g Pasta

100g broccoli

Quickie pan-fried salmon

Method

Peeling the carrots — watch your fingers!

1   Wash and dry the salmon fillets. Sprinkle both sides with all purpose seasoning, curry powder and dry herbs, then leave to stand.

2   Add 1 litre of water to a saucepan and bring to the boil, add a pinch of salt and a dash of olive oil.

3   In the meantime, peel the carrots, wash and slice into finger length strips then add to a separate small pan of cold water and bring to the boil for 10 minutes.

4   Add 400g of pasta to the litre of boiling water, then reduce the heat and simmer for 10 minutes or until al dente.

5   Whilst the pasta and carrots are boiling, wash the broccoli and remove the stalks then add to the saucepan of carrots for 6 minutes.

If your salmon has skin, ask an adult to skin it for you.

6   Add the olive oil to the frying pan, then the garlic paste. When the oil is hot, add the salmon fillets and cook for 10 minutes (turning after 5 minutes). The pasta will be ready first. Drain into a colander then return to the pan.

7   Add the pasta sauce to the already hot pasta and stir before serving on 4 separate plates. Drain the carrots and broccoli and serve with the pasta. Serve the salmon with the pasta and vegetables.

The salmon sprinkled with its seasoning.

children are the heart of everything we do°

Alyssa, 8, provided us with this delicious recipe, that can be altered to include white chocolate or dates, depending on what you like. Alyssa likes healthy self-sustaining foods and says this dish 'has a unique flavour and is brilliant for a snack'.

Alyssa Kingston-Miles

Tom Kerridge

Alyssa & Tom

Dairy-free apricot rock cakes

Dairy-free apricot rock cakes

Tom competed and won the main course round of BB2's Great British Menu 2010 and is regularly featured in the papers for his restaurant The Hand & Flowers, where he has won a Michelin Star.

Measuring the flour using the weighing scales.

Stirring the apricots and sugar into the flour.

Chef's comments

Alyssa's dairy-free rock cakes have the appeal of a great cake but also looking for a health point of view; they are dairy-free and are given beautiful sweet richness with the addition of apricots.

Tom Kerridge

children are the heart of everything we do

Alyssa & Tom

Dairy-free apricot rock cakes

100g dried apricots

Makes 12 cakes

15 minutes cooking time

. . . .

Ingredients

100g dried apricots

250g self-raising flour

125g soya margarine

75g caster sugar

2-3 tablespoons soya milk

1 egg

Self-raising flour

Eggs

Method

1 Set the oven to 180°C/Gas Mark 4/350°F.

2 Snip the apricots into small pieces.

3 Add the flour and butter into a bowl and rub together to make breadcrumbs. Stir in the sugar and apricots.

4 Add the egg and mix in enough milk to make a soft lumpy mixture.

5 Using spoons divide the mixture into 10 cakes and place on an oiled baking sheet.

6 Bake in the oven for 12–15 minutes until golden brown and firm to the touch.

7 Place on a wire rack to cool. Eat and enjoy!

Breaking the eggs into the flour.

Spooning the mixture into the baking tray.

Dairy-free apricot rock cakes.

Shaping the rock cakes.

I love this recipe as it is easy to make and tastes superb. I would like to have dinner with the Queen, and my favourite kitchen tool is the mixing bowl full of leftover chocolate! Maybe I could share it with her?

Mitch Tonks

Mitch Tonks

Strawberry meringue delight

Mitch is passionate about British seafood and its conservation. He runs three restaurants, is a well-known chef and food writer, and has recently launched the first i-Pad app dedicated to seafood.

Strawberry meringue delight

For 6 people
5 minutes cooking time
. . . .

Ingredients

Ready to use meringue nests
Squirty fresh cream
Punnet of strawberries
White and milk cooking chocolate
Decorative chocolate stars
Green gelatine

Chef's comments

I love the way that he has used readily available ingredients and then chosen to make some effort on the presentation, things like dipping the strawberries in chocolate so that the flavours are together on every bite make a difference.

Mitch Tonks

Method

1 Wash six well-shaped strawberries and slice through to near the top of the strawberries. Spread the sliced strawberries to form a fan-shape.

2 Heat and melt the milk and white chocolate.

3 Dip the strawberries three-quarters of the way from the tip into the chocolate and allow them to drip and cool. Repeat with the white chocolate.

4 Fill the meringue nests with the cream and lay strawberry slices on the top of each nest.

5 Place tiny decorative stars onto the chocolate; milk chocolate stars onto the white chocolate, white chocolate stars onto the milk chocolate.

6 Cut a leaf and stalk shape from the gelatine and place at the end of the strawberry. You can also drizzle chocolate on top. Keep refrigerated until ready to eat.

Quick, easy and delicious!

Katie, 15, loved cooking with our chef Chris Lee, and has been invited to come and cook in his restaurant kitchen! If she could invite anyone for dinner it would be her mum, so she could cook her favourite chicken pasta dish.

Katie Kennedy

Katie & Chris

Katie's samosas

Chris Lee

Easy to make and fab to eat.

Chris is the Head Chef of The Bildeston Crown in Suffolk, which he runs with his wife Hayley. The restaurant has 3 AA rosettes to its name, as well as a number of other awards.

Chef's comments

What do you think chef? Delicious.

Katie has the makings of a great cook. Already very competent with this dish, she was delighted the difference made by the thinner pastry. Katie was great fun and there is indeed an open invitation to visit us in Suffolk.

Chris Lee

children are the heart of everything we do°

Katie & Chris

Katie's samosas

Potatoes

Makes 15
20 minutes cooking time

· ·

Ingredients

Filo pastry sheets
Petit pois
2 large potatoes, cooked and mashed
2 tsp medium curry powder
1 egg

Filo pastry sheets

Katie's samosas

Method

1. Preheat the oven to 180°C/Gas Mark 4/350°F. Mix together the potatoes and peas, and add in the curry powder.

2. Cut the pastry into fifteen 4 inch strips.

3. Beat the egg and brush the pastry sheets, do this by layering 4 sheets of filo pastry on top of each other brushing in between each sheet.

4. Spoon a little of the mixture near the bottom left corner of the pastry and begin to fold over into triangular shapes, until you come to the end of the strips.

5. Place on a greased and lined baking tray and brush the samosa with a little egg.

6. Cook in the oven for 15–20 mins until flaky and golden brown.

Mixing together the ingredients for the filling.

Folding the samosas into triangular shapes.

Arranging the samosas on a long serving plate.

Shaping the samosas and seal with beaten egg.

43

Dylan, 16, created this risotto as a simple dish that saves wasting food, is delicious and contains lots of vegetables. He usually likes anything with pasta, but this risotto dish is the perfect alternative to pasta dishes.

Dylan Forbes

Dylan & Mitch

Sunday leftover risotto

Mitch Tonks

Mitch is passionate about British seafood and its conservation. He runs three restaurants, is a well-known chef and food writer, and has recently launched the first i-Pad app dedicated to seafood.

Re-creating my dish in a professional kitchen was fun.

Chef's comments

Service please!

This is a good wholesome dish that will keep all the family happy. I like the fact that Dylan has thought about using leftovers and is relaxed about what these might be, the dish will be different every time and that is a good way to work out what you like and what tastes good together.

Mitch Tonks

children are the heart of everything we do

Dylan & Mitch

Sunday leftover risotto

onion

For 4 people
30 minutes cooking time

. . . .

Ingredients

Bacon
Risotto rice
Vegetable oil
Worcester sauce
Stock cube
Tin of chopped tomatoes
Chopped onion
Any leftover meat from a Sunday roast
Any leftover vegetables
Apple sauce or stuffing if possible
Tomato puree
Grated cheese to serve

Vegetables

Sunday leftover risotto

Sunday leftover risotto

Method

1 Fry the onion and bacon in a little oil until soft.

2 Add a tablespoon of the tomato puree and blend in.

3 Add the rice and any cooked leftover vegetables.

4 Cut the meat into cubes and add to the mixture.

5 Pour over enough stock to cover and add Worcester sauce to taste.

6 Simmer for half an hour until thoroughly hot, the meat is heated through and stock has evaporated.

7 Serve with a sprinkle of grated cheese.

Peeling the onion.

Adding cooked leftover vegetables to the frying pan.

I added a sprig of basil for decoration.

Garnishing with grated cheese.

children are the heart of everything we do

Charly, 8, made this beautiful pudding which is 'yummy' warm or cold. The best recipe she has cooked has been Banana Pie, another sweet dish that is nice to have as a treat.

Charly

Charly & Shaun

Lemon curd crumble

Shaun Rankin

Shaun has worked as a chef in restaurants from Chicago to Australia, and the Mayfair Hotel in London, and now runs Bohemia on the island of Jersey. He has retained a Michelin star for 7 years.

Making the pastry can be sticky fun.

Chef's comments

This recipe is really simple and fun to make. Lemon and chocolate is a truly great combination that never seems to fail whether its lunch, dinner or a tea time treat! One of the great things about this dessert is the crunchy texture of the crumble topping.

Shaun Rankin

Pretty as a picture but even better to eat.

49

children are the heart of everything we do

Charly & Shaun

Lemon curd crumble

For 6 people
25 minutes cooking time

. . . .

Ingredients

200g plain and self-raising flour
(100g of each)
100g margarine
25g sugar
Cold water or milk to mix for dough
Lemon curd

Crumble mix

100g self-raising flour
50g margarine
50g sugar

Lemon curd

Sugar

Making the crumble mix.

Lemon curd crumble

Method

1 Preheat the oven to 190°C/Gas Mark 5/375°F.

2 Mix flour and sugar in a bowl. Rub in the margarine using hands.

3 Then add just enough milk or water to form the dough to roll out.

4 Roll out, place in the a flan dish, cut to size.

5 Then spoon the lemon curd on and spread out as thin or as thick as you like.

6 Rub together all the crumble ingredients then add on top.

7 Put in the oven and bake for 25 minutes or until golden.

Rubbing the margarine, flour and sugar to make the dough.

Spooning the lemon curd onto the base.

Lemon curd crumble

Cooks & Kids

children are the heart of everything we do®

Shane, 16, created this fantastic-looking dish using chicken, as he says it tastes good. Shane's most successful recipe ever was an orange and chocolate cheesecake, but this may just have beaten it!

Shane McAllister

Shane & Gill

Chicken breast with mozzarella & pancetta

Chicken breast with mozzarella & pancetta

Gill Moss

Gill is a sous chef at De Vere Venues. Her favourite food is anything sweet containing chocolate! Gill also won the recent De Vere 'cooking with verve' academy.

Assembling the dish to restaurant standard.

Chef's comments

This is a lovely homely dish that would impress anyone, Shane has done a great job on presentation and it looks delicious! I would cook this for my family and friends on their birthdays or special occasions, it's sure to be a big hit!

Gill Moss

Seeing my dish presented this way has given me inspiration.

children are the heart of everything we do©

Shane & Gill

Chicken breast with mozzarella & pancetta

Aubergine

For 2 people
30 minutes cooking time
. . . .

Ingredients

2 chicken breast fillets
1 pack of mozzarella
1 pack of pancetta/streaky bacon
1 large potato
1 large tomato
1 aubergine
1 red onion

Pancetta or streaky bacon

Chicken breast with mozzarella & pancetta

Method

1 Preheat the oven to 180°C/Gas Mark 4/350°F.

2 Cut a pocket into the thick end of the chicken fillets and stuff with the chopped mozzarella.

3 Wrap the chicken fillets in the pancetta and place on a sheet of tin foil on a baking tray.

4 Put the fillets into the oven and cook for about 20 minutes.

5 Grate the potato and onion, and mix together. Using circular biscuit cutters, shape the potato into rosti shapes, and then fry in a saucepan until golden brown.

6 Slice the aubergine and tomato into 1 cm slices and lightly grill.

7 Stack them on top of one another and serve with the cooked chicken breast.

Chopping the onion for the potato rosti.

Grate the potato.

Slicing the aubergine with a sharp knife. Be careful!

> I made this delicious milky dessert and I love the fact it is cold and tasty. It's perfect for parties in the summer for cooling down with, and takes very little preparation. An ideal treat!

Bryn Williams

Bryn Williams

Jelly cream

Welsh chef Bryn has worked with some of London's top chefs, including Marco Pierre-White and Michel Roux, before opening his own restaurant Odette's to critical acclaim.

Ingredients

For 4-6 people

I packet of jelly
Tin of evaporated milk
Boiling water

Method

1 Dissolve the jelly into boiling water.

2 Leave until half set.

3 Combine the jelly and evaporated milk.

4 Beat well and transfer to the mould to finish setting.

5 When set decorate with cream, chocolate shavings, fruit or leave plain.

Chef's comments

This is a good idea for making jelly a bit different! I think fresh strawberries would be nice served with this too. Hopefully, as he gets older and his cooking skills develop, he'll start making jelly from scratch which is great fun.

Bryn Williams

Measuring out the jelly crystals. or you can use a packet of jelly.

Chocolate Quickies are my favourite food and I love cooking them for my mum. If I was stranded on a desert island, I would take sausages, mashed potatoes, pizza, chocolate and some ice cream to keep me cool.

Gill Moss

Gill Moss

Choc quickies

Gill is a sous chef at De Vere Venues. Her favourite food is anything sweet containing chocolate! Gill also won the recent De Vere 'cooking with verve' academy.

Method

1 Break or crush the biscuits into pieces about the size of a small finger.

2 Grease a 7" square tin.

3 Melt the margarine, sugar and syrup in a pan. When melted together add the cocoa powder.

4 Allow to boil for 1 minute, stirring all the time.

5 Remove from the heat and stir in the biscuits.

6 Put the mixture in the greased tin and press down.

7 Melt the chocolate in a heatproof dish over boiling water.

8 Beat until smooth and pour over the biscuit mix.

9 Chill in the refrigerator until firm, and cut into pieces.

Makes 12
. . . .

Ingredients

4oz margarine
2 tbsp cocoa powder
1 tbsp Demerara sugar
2 tbsp syrup
8oz Rich Tea biscuits
4oz plain cooking chocolate

Chef's comments

These yummy choc cookies are fantastic; these are great when your friends come over to watch a DVD, or a special gift to keep on the right side of your teacher! These choc quickies are making my mouth water... I think I'm going to have cup of tea and a choc quickie!

Gill Moss

Delicious Choc quickies — don't they look yummy!

children are the heart of everything we do

Megan, 10, would like to cook this dish for her favourite singers JLS, and I think they'd definitely enjoy it! This potato and cheese dish is perfect with a light salad, or as an accompaniment to a main meal.

Megan Webb

Megan & Matt

Potato-licious

Matt Tebbutt

Matt runs the Foxhunter in Abergavenny, and is a passionate supporter of local seasonal produce. He is well-known as the guest-presenter on Saturday Kitchen on BBC I.

Peeling the skin off the mushrooms can be fiddly.

Chef's comments

This recipe is filling and tasty and so easy for kids to put together. It is ideal for a quick lunch or as an accompaniment to grilled chicken for a great supper dish. Kids can have fun experimenting with this recipe and try adding herbs or different types of cheese.

Matt Tebbutt

Warm, gooey, potato-cheesy loveliness.

children are the heart of everything we do

Megan & Matt

Potato-licious

Potatoes

For 2 people
10 minutes cooking time

Ingredients

2 large potatoes, peeled and cut
   into small chunks
4 slices of smoked bacon, cut into
   small pieces
Half a small onion, peeled and
   chopped finely
2 flat mushrooms or 6 button
   mushrooms, cut into small pieces
Half a teaspoon full of mixed herbs
100g grated cheese

Mushrooms and onion

Grated cheese

Method

1 Boil the water and put the potato chunks into the saucepan, boil for 10 minutes.

2 Heat a tablespoon of oil in a frying pan and add the bacon pieces.

3 Fry for two minutes and then add the mushrooms, onion and herbs and cook until the mushrooms are soft and the onions clear in colour.

4 Drain the potatoes and put in a bowl.

5 Add the cooked bacon, mushroom, onion, herbs and grated cheese to the potatoes in the bowl, and gently mix together.

6 Serve in bowls.

Carefully chopping the mushrooms with a sharp knife.

Frying the mushrooms in a saucepan.

Potato-licious

Topping with grated cheese. I also added chives as a garnish.

children are the heart of everything we do

Evan, 6, and Keya, 8, loved making these pasties, saying that this was the most successful recipe they had cooked! These yummy home-cooked pasties are great for eating on the go, but be careful of the hot filling.

Keya & Evan Dalby

Lisa Allen

Keya, Evan & Lisa

Baked bean pastie

Lisa Allen, star of BBC2's Great British Menu, was the first woman chef to reach the finals of the competition. She is Head Chef at the Northcote, in Blackburn.

Baked bean pastie

Method

1 Preheat the oven to 220°C/Gas Mark 7/425°F.

2 Chop the onion and cut the bacon into small pieces with scissors.

3 Fry the onion until soft and add the bacon to the pan.

4 When cooked, put into a large bowl, add the beans, and Worcestershire sauce and cubed cheese if using, and mix well.

5 Roll out the pastry and cut four squares from each slab. This will create eight large pasties, you can create minis if you'd prefer.

6 Spoon the mixture evenly onto the pastry and press the edges together to make a seam in the centre of each.

7 Place on a baking sheet, brush with milk and bake for 15-20 minutes until puffed and golden-brown.

Makes 8
20 minutes cooking time

Ingredients

2 tins of beans
1 pack of bacon/ham
1 large onion
2 sheets of puff pastry
Milk for brushing
Dash of olive oil
Cubed cheese – optional
Worcester sauce – optional

Chef's comments

If you love baked beans this is something you must try; a little different from beans on toast – flaky pastry, warm and delicious, it's a meal in one, very simple to produce and lots of fun to make!

Lisa Allen

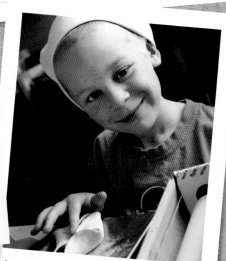

Press the edges together to make a seam in the centre.

65

Kylie, 16, sent this recipe to us, but says she eats 10 bananas a week! With all of that healthy eating, a pineapple upsidedown cake is the perfect treat.

Kylie & Stephen

Pineapple upsidedown cake

Stephen Terry

Stephen earned his first Michelin star at 25 and has worked in restaurants in London, Paris and St Tropez. After gaining a Michelin Star at The Walnut Tree, he opened The Hardwick, near Abergavenny.

Putting the mixture in an ovenproof dish.

Chef's comments

My pineapple upsidedown cake is ready to enjoy.

This is one of my very favourite puddings! Glace cherries in the base with the pineapple chunks is very colourful and try serving it with coconut ice cream for a totally tropical experience.

Stephen Terry

67

children are the heart of everything we do

Kylie & Stephen

Pineapple upsidedown cake

For 4–6 people
15 minutes cooking time

Ingredients

2 oz butter
2 oz brown sugar
1 can pineapple chunks
½ tbsp self-raising flour
¼ level tbsp salt
¼ lb butter
¼ lb caster sugar
Finely grated peel of 1 lemon
3 eggs
4–5 tbsp milk

Pineapple chunks

Lemon peel

Pineapple upsidedown cake

Method

1. Preheat the oven to 175°C/Gas Mark 4/350°F. For the topping, put the pineapple into a mixing bowl.

2. Melt the butter, add the sugar and pour this over the pineapple. Set aside.

3. For the base, add the flour, butter, salt and sugar in a bowl and mix together.

4. Add the lemon peel, 3 eggs and 5 tablespoons of milk and mix thoroughly.

5. Put the mixture evenly into 4-6 ramekins and cook for 15 minutes.

6. After 15 minutes, stick a fork through the centre of the cakes to check if they are cooked.

7. Afterwards, leave the cakes to cool down for 10 minutes and then serve them with custard or cream.

I'm using fresh pineapple. Don't forget to remove the eyelets.

The topping goes at the bottom.

And then the milk.

Adding the eggs to make the cake mixture.

children are the heart of everything we do

Ythan has created this delicious dessert, using pears and chocolate. It's lovely to use pears in cooking, not simply being eaten as a snack. This is great for impressing your friends!

Ythan Johnson

Ythan & Tom

Chocolate & pear surprise

Tom Kerridge

Tom competed and won the main course round of BB2's Great British Menu and is regularly featured in the papers for his restaurant The Hand & Flowers, where he has won a Michelin Star.

Making chocolate custard to pour over the surprise.

Chef's comments

Chocolate heaven on a plate.

Ythan's chocolate and pear surprise looks a fantastic dish. The flavour is a classic combination that works very well together, and the chocolate custard gives that added bit of luxury.

Tom Kerridge

Ythan & Tom

Chocolate & pear surprise

For 6 people
20 minutes cooking time

Ingredients

For the brownies

140g/5oz dark or milk chocolate

225g/8oz unsalted butter

200g flour

5 free range eggs

450g/1lb caster sugar

110g/4oz cocoa powder

25g/1oz milk chocolate drops

25g/1oz white chocolate drops

For the chocolate custard

1 carton of good quality custard

2 tbsp cocoa powder

4 ripe pears peeled and chopped

Dessicated coconut

Eggs and pears

Chocolate

Chocolate & pear surprise

Method

1 Heat the oven to 180°C/Gas mark 4/ 350°F. Grease 6 ramekins or small ring moulds with butter.

2 Melt the butter and the caster gently together in a large saucepan.

3 Take the pan off the heat and beat in the chocolate, eggs, flour and the cocoa powder.

4 Divide ¾ of the chopped pears and all of the chocolate mixture between your 6 ramekins or ring moulds, bake in oven 15-20 minutes until the top is firm but inside is soft.

5 Leave for 5 minutes before turning out onto a wire cooling rack.

6 Take the custard and the cocoa powder and pour into a bowl. Beat thoroughly.

7 Spoon a little custard on top of the brownies, (just enough to cover the tops).

8 Pour some pieces of the chopped pear on top. To finish pour more custard over the pears.

9 Sprinkle some of the desiccated coconut over the top.

Grease the ring moulds with butter.

Using a whisk helps the cocoa powder mix into the custard easier.

Careful with that hot saucepan!

Chloe must have lots of friends when she makes birthday cakes like these! Great for celebrating with friends, but don't eat too many slices — it's a once-a-year treat. Use different types of fruit for different flavours.

Chloe McKinsley

Lisa Allen

Chloe & Lisa

Birthday cake

Lisa Allen, star of BBC2's Great British Menu, was the first woman chef to reach the finals of the competition. She is Head Chef at the Northcote, in Blackburn.

35 minutes cooking time

Ingredients

175g butter
100g cocoa powder
12 eggs
350g sugar
200g plain flour
100ml double cream
Yoghurt and fruit

Caught finishing off the cake mixture.

Method

1 Heat the oven to 180°C/Gas Mark 4/350°F. Grease and line a deep cake tin.

2 Separate the egg yolks and whisk them with the sugar.

3 Whisk the egg whites.

4 Sift the flour and cocoa powder together.

5 Melt the butter.

6 Fold it all together until smooth and airy. Bake for 35 minutes.

7 When cool cut the cake lengthways and add the filling.

8 Whip the double cream and add to the yoghurt which needs to be set. Decorate the cake with the set mixture and the fruit.

Chef's comments

What can I say!? Chocolate is a favourite for most of us, children and adults alike – great fun to make and even better to eat, kids love it and especially when they get to lick the bowl clean!

Lisa Allen

Jamie, aged 9 says these are his favourite biscuits. He loves making them for his friends. They are especially nice with strawberries or raspberries so you don't eat too many!

Jamie Telford

John Woodward

John is Executive Head Chef for the De Vere Venues and arranged all of the cookery days for the children, as well as providing his culinary expertise!

Jamie & John

Choco-boom cookies

Method

1 Preheat oven to 180°C/Gas Mark 4/350°F. Lightly grease a baking tray. Beat the butter and icing sugar into a mixing bowl until light and fluffy.

2 Beat in the vanilla flavouring or the grated orange rind. Beat in the flour to form a dough. Use you fingers to add the last of the flour.

3 Divide the dough into two equal pieces and beat the melted chocolate into one half. Keeping each half of the dough separate, cover and leave to chill for about 30 minutes.

4 Roll the chocolate mixture into a neat rectangle shape and roll the white mixture into a long sausage shape. Both should be the same length as one another.

5 Brush some beaten egg over the chocolate mixture on one side only, place the white mixture on top then roll the chocolate mixture tightly around the white mixture.

6 Cut the block into equal slices and place each flat on the baking tray, leaving space between each to allow them to expand slightly whilst cooking.

7 Cook for about 10 minutes until just firm. Leave to cool completely and enjoy.

Ingredients

Makes 18
10 minutes cooking time

175g/6oz butter
75g/2³⁄₄oz/6 tbsp icing sugar
1 tsp vanilla extract or the grated rind of ¹⁄₂ orange
250g/9oz of plain flour
25g/1oz dark chocolate, melted
A little beaten egg

Chef's comments

These delightful little biscuits taste great and are so moreish! Crisp on the outside and soft-centred you can really taste the orange running through the rich chocolate.

John Woodward

These will be a big hit at parties.

77

children are the heart of everything we do°

Craig provided this traditional Scottish dish whilst cooking at Cameron House, near Loch Lomond. He likes the recipe as it contains sausages, and told our chefs that 'they were the best'. Glad you enjoyed the day Craig!

Craig Rowan

Craig & Chris

Stovies

Chris Lee

Chris is the Head Chef of The Bildeston Crown in Suffolk, which he runs with his wife Hayley. The restaurant has 3 AA rosettes to its name, as well as a number of other awards.

Now for the best bit – the taste test.

Chef's comments

These children are cooking from the heart. The recipes chosen reflect what they enjoy to eat – in Craig's case it is clearly sausages - and this enjoyment comes through in the taste. Well done Craig!

Chris Lee

A true Scottish dish served eloquently.

children are the heart of everything we do

Craig & Chris

Stovies

For 4 people
45 minutes cooking time

························

Ingredients

500g / 1lb 2oz of potatoes
1 large onion, peeled
2 carrots, peeled
1 small turnip, peeled
10 link sausages or square sausage
     (dependent on availability)
2 beef stock cubes made into a
     tea cup of stock
Salt and pepper to taste
Dash of Worcester sauce

Ingredients

Stovies

Method

1 Chop and dice the potatoes into bite sizes and cut the onion into rings.

2 Add some thickly chopped carrot and turnip into a large pot.

3 Cut the sausages into 4 / 5 pieces each and insert these into the pot also.

4 Add hot water to the pot and cover the ingredients, put the lid on the pot and cook on the hob slowly for about 35 minutes or until potatoes and turnip are tender.

5 Season with salt and pepper and add the stock and Worcester sauce to the pot, cook for a further 10 minutes.

6 The stovies can now be served in a bowl.

Half a kilo of potatoes – that's a lot of peeling.

Mixing the vegetables together in the pot.

Stovies can be served on their own but also delicious with a Yorkshire Pudding.

children are the heart of everything we do°

Taliesin, 9, says he chose this recipe to cook as it is comfort food and good for winter evenings. His favourite chef is Michael Roux Jr, and his five items for a desert island would be cucumbers, chocolate, watermelon, a Cornish pasty and steak, because it is succulent.

Taliesin Bourne

Taliesin & Matt

Tuna crunch

Method

1. Preheat the oven to 175°C/Gas Mark 4/350°F. Put the milk, flour and butter into a saucepan. Melt the butter and keep stirring until the sauce has thickened.

2. Turn down the heat and simmer for 2 minutes Add the drained tins of tuna to the sauce and stir occasionally to prevent sticking.

3. Meanwhile in a microwaveable dish, melt some extra butter. Cut the bread into small squares and stir into the butter.

4. Pour the sauce and tuna into an ovenproof dish and put the buttered bread on top to form a crust. Bake for 20 minutes.

5. Serve with potatoes and peas or sweetcorn.

Matt Tebbutt

Matt runs the Foxhunter in Abergavenny, and is a passionate supporter of local seasonal produce. He is well-known as the guest-presenter on Saturday Kitchen on BBC 1.

For 4 people
20 minutes cooking time

Ingredients

2 tins of tuna
2 slices of bread
300ml milk
20g butter
30ml plain flour
Extra butter for melting
Peas, sweetcorn and mash potatoes
    to serve

Chef's comments

Its great to see the kids showing an interest in cooking and choosing their favourite recipes. Food should be fun and taste good but should also get the kids involved in where their food comes from and how its prepared.

Matt Tebbutt

children are the heart of everything we do

Lachlan and Jack created this wonderful soup, with a lovely rich colour. With beetroot, carrot and apple it makes a lovely winter warming meal, served with some crusty bread.

John Woodward

John is Executive Head Chef for the De Vere Venues and arranged all of the cookery days for the children, as well as providing his culinary expertise!

Lachlan, Jack & John

Beetroot & apple soup

Chef's comments

Cook for 1 hour, until the beetroot is soft.

What a lovely fresh, tasty soup this is with a little twist. Really easy to make you get a deep flavour and colour from the beetroot and the sweetness of the apple really works. Perfect for dinner parties, a light lunch or winter warmer on a cold winters day. Really healthy too with virtually no fat so you can eat even more!!!

John Woodward

Method

For 4 people
1 hour cooking time

Ingredients

4 fresh beetroot
1 onion
1 carrot
1 clove of garlic
1 Bramley apple
1 vegetable stock cube mixed with
    500ml warm water
50g mixed dried herbs

1 Wash and peel the vegetables, then dice into cubes.

2 Fry the onion until soft and add the beetroot, carrot and garlic.

3 Peel, core and dice the apples and add to the mixture. Add the stock and herbs.

4 Add the pepper to taste and cook for approximately 1 hour, until the beetroot is soft.

5 Blend the soup and add more black pepper if needed. Serve with a swirl of cream.

Amy's porridge recipe is a super-healthy way to begin the day! We've added chocolate in the picture, but for breakfast, why not add a spoonful of honey to add sweetness?

Amy Gough

Shaun Rankin

Amy & Shaun

Fruity porridge

Shaun has worked as a chef in restaurants from Chicago to Australia, and the Mayfair Hotel in London, and now runs Bohemia on the island of Jersey. He has retained a Michelin star for 7 years.

For 4 people
10 minutes cooking time

Ingredients

1 cup of porridge oats
2 cups of whole fat milk
Handful of raisins
2 bananas

Add any fruit you like.

Method

1 Pour the oats and milk into a saucepan and add in the raisins. Stir everything well.

2 Heat the mixture on a medium heat stirring throughout and bring to the boil.

3 Turn the heat down and simmer until the mixture thickens, stirring continuously.

4 Pour the porridge into bowls.

5 Slice the banana and place on top.

Chef's comments

What a great way to start the day. This recipe is full of healthy nutrients and vitamins. The great thing about this dish is that you can use any fruit you wish to and you can create great combinations using different flavours such as nuts, honey and yoghurt.

Shaun Rankin

Porridge is yummy when served with fresh fruit.

De Vere recipes

Cream of wild mushroom soup

30 minutes cooking time
. . . .

Ingredients

100g wild mushrooms
100g button mushrooms
1 white onion
200 ml vegetable stock
200 ml cream
Butter
Few sprigs parsley
Seasoning

Method

1 Wash the mushrooms getting rid of any dirt or grit.

2 Dice the onion and fry in a little butter.

3 Add the mushrooms and cook until soft.

4 Add the warm vegetable stock. Bring to the boil and simmer for 30 minutes.

5 Wash and chop the parsley and keep to one side.

6 Liquidise the soup, pass through a sieve and add salt and pepper if desired.

7 Serve with a drizzle of cream and chopped parsley, and some crusty bread.

Scone-based pizza

For 4 people
20 minutes cooking time

Ingredients

110g self raising flour
25g butter or margarine
50g cheddar cheese
Torn basil leaves
4 tbsp milk
1 large tbsp tomato puree
2 tbsp water

For the topping

Choose your favourite toppings such as ham and pineapple or cheese and basil

Method

1 Pre heat the oven to 200°C/Gas Mark 6/400°F.

2 In a large mixing bowl rub the butter and flour until it resembles fine breadcrumbs.

3 Tear 3 large basil leaves into the mixture and add the grated cheese.

4 Slowly add the milk to bring all the dry ingredients together.

5 Roll out the scone mixture on a floured surface to approximately 1.5cm.

6 Mix the tomato puree with the water in a cup and then spread evenly over the pizza base.

7 Top with your favourite toppings and cheese.

8 Bake in the oven for 15 to 20 minutes.

89

children are the heart of everything we do

Salmon pasta

Method

Ingredients

6oz salmon fillet

Pinch of cracked black pepper

250g plain flour

A handful of spinach

330ml double cream

100ml white wine vinegar

Seasoning

100ml butter

100ml olive oil

1 Blanch the spinach and blitz to make a paste.

2 Season the salmon, place in a little water and poach in oven for 15 mins (180°C/Gas Mark 4/ 350°F).

3 Put the pasta in boiling salted water and cook until done.

4 Add cream to the white wine vinegar and boil. Whisk in the butter until slightly thickened.

5 Drain the pasta, season and dress with the sauce, olive oil and pepper.

6 Place the salmon fillet on top of the pasta and serve.

Peanut butter and strawberry jam cookies

Ingredients

100g unsalted butter
175g smooth peanut butter
150g caster sugar
115g plain flour
1 egg yolk
200g strawberry jam

Method

1 Preheat oven to 180°C/Gas Mark 4/ 350°F.

2 Beat together (with a electric mixer) the unsalted butter, along with the smooth peanut butter and the caster sugar, mix until light and fluffy, then add the plain flour and 1 egg yolk.

3 Wrap into cling film and refrigerate for up to 2 hours.

4 To bake, take the dough and place onto baking tray with parchment paper into 1inch balls, flatten the balls slightly and make a thumbprint in the middle of the dough, fill each one with strawberry jam.

5 Bake in oven til the edges start to lightly brown, for 10-12 mins.

6 Once finished, place onto a wired cooling rack and cool, and lightly dust with icing sugar.

children are the heart of everything we do

The people and chefs who made Cooks & Kids possible

A huge thank you to the people who donated their time and talent to help to produce Cooks & Kids. Here's a little about the team:

Photographers

MPP Image Creation Limited

Miranda founded MPP Image Creation in 1992 for clients in the event sector. They cover anything from private parties to international conferences. She says:

"When I realised Cooks & Kids was the brainchild of the National Fostering Agency, how could I resist? I don't want to make a big thing out of this, but I was adopted as a child so immediately felt a natural empathy with the project. The day itself was great fun. The kids were very comfortable and we laughed a lot. A memorable day, great kids and a fantastic project!"

www.mppimagecreation.com

Martin Stock

Martin is a freelance photographer, covering corporate events, architectural photographs and weddings. He says:

"In all honesty, I found the whole experience of covering the Cooks & Kids day at Cameron House, Scotland extremely uplifting! The children themselves were an absolute delight and I hope I have captured in my photography their excitement as they worked with the chefs to make their recipes come to glorious life."

www.mnsphotography.com

Simon Broadhead

Simon has been a UK based full time professional photographer for over 25 years, specialising in the photography of people, food, architecture and interiors. He says:

"What a fabulous day! Seeing the joy and happiness between the children, the chefs and their

parents during our special day together, was a real eye opener to a world that often seems a million miles away from ours. I really hope this book helps potential future foster parents to see how rewarding and fulfilling fostering really is."

www.shoot360.co.uk

Lisa Knight

Lisa took her first photography qualification aged 15, and she is now a freelance photographer, available for commissions of portraits, events, and commercial photography. Lisa says:

"As a foster career I appreciate the importance of working with Looked After Children to show them how good life can be. Many children in care have little self-belief, so working with them to show they are valid individuals is a huge part of equipping them for their future. If in any small way I have helped in the process, it makes me extremely proud!"

www.whiterosestudios.co.uk

The people and chefs who made Cooks & Kids possible

Nutrition

Sodexo

Sodexo provided Cooks & Kids with the nutritional information. They were the first food services company to make a public commitment to encourage healthy lifestyles through good food. Through their Healthwise campaign they made huge changes to the way children eat. With over 55 years experience working in schools, providing millions of meals every week for children, Sodexo were ideal for providing information for children to help them make informed decisions about food and health.

Website designers

STEEL

A word from our website creators:

"Hi! We're STEEL, a London-based digital agency. When the NFA approached us to create the Cooks & Kids website we jumped at the chance to help them with this fantastic, charitable venture.

Our challenge was to create a fun and engaging website that would

create lots of digital buzz. You can take a look at our handy work at www.cooksandkids.com. The site features sample recipes, info on the chefs involved and a blog with all the latest publicity info and promotions.

The website was designed by Nicola Bowden of STEEL and the site was built by Mark Harris – a great friend of STEEL. Everyone involved donated their time for free to support Cooks & Kids and Magic Breakfast.

WRG

WRG have been involved in the Cooks & Kids project through the procurement of the photographers for each of the cookery days. We are also responsible for the production of a video diary to showcase the activities that took place at each of the cookery day locations.

Graffeg

Graffeg provided the book design, editorial and production expertise and would like to thank the whole team for their efforts including Sarah Evans who helped NFA edit the entire book.

Budding little cooks turning into professional chefs.

Working with the chefs was a great experience.

All the children were pleased with their dishes.

children are the heart of everything we do

The people and chefs who made Cooks & Kids possible

Children

Rebecca
Georgia Sutherland-Jones
Macie French
Amber
Alyssa Kingston-Miles
Katie Kennedy
Dylan Forbes
Charly
Shane McAllister
Megan Webb
Keya & Evan Dalby
Kylie
Ythan Johnson
Chloe McKinsley
Jamie Telford
Craig Rowan
Taliesin Bourne
Lachlan & Jack
Amy Gough

NFA Staff

The staff at NFA who worked tirelessly to make this book happen:
Alan Rustad
Andrew Isaac
Michael Stewart
Laura Watkins
Liz Cowling
Christine Gale

Louise Bouckley
Veronica Purser
Millicent Otoo
Sonia Polden
Cilla Camillo
Mandy White
Katie Tomlin
Sue Cheung
Fiona Barnes
Suzanne Robson

Parents / foster carers

Rosie Lake
Debbie & Mark Gill
Julie & Gary Johnson
Tracy Sutherland
Sandy Hughes
Julie Gough
Eleanor Harding
Teresa Chesterman
Annie & Stephen Adair
Richard French
Avis Pearce
David Rowan
Vera Middleton
Val & Brian Eldridge
Roni Kingston-Miles
Avis Pearce
Hugh Lake
Vanessa & Mark Dalby
Julia & Richard Baker
Emma & Hywel Evans

De Vere chefs

Mark Scobbie

Kieran Whyte

The people and chefs who made Cooks & Kids possible

Donna Nudd

Mark owen

Jamian Lewis

Matt Gardener

Iain Dickson

Darren Foster

Kelly Snowdon

James Hawtin

Darren Kennedy

Index